Enduring the Course

Parental guide to increase understanding, reduce stigma, and expand intervention options when mental health concerns arise

Ebonyjae, LISW-S

©*2020* by Ebony Hull | Steward Publishing. All Rights Reserved.

ISBN: 9798687006682

Steward Publishing, LTD.

🌐 stewardpublishing.org

No part of this publication may be reproduced, stored in a retrieval system or transmitted, in any form or by any means electronic, mechanical, photocopying, recording or otherwise without prior written permission from the publisher, except for the inclusion of brief quotations in a review.

Disclaimer

No part of this publication may be reproduced or transmitted in any form or by any means, mechanical or electronic, including photocopying or recording, or by any information storage and retrieval system, or transmitted by email without permission in writing from the author.

Neither the author nor the publisher assumes any responsibility for errors, omissions, or contrary interpretations of the subject matter herein. Any perceived slight of any individual or organization is purely unintentional.

Brand and product names are trademarks or registered trademarks of their respective owners.

Table of Contents

Dedication 7

Foreword. 9

Enduring the Course 11

Introduction 13

A Basis of Understanding 23

Mental health and the Church 31

Managing the Mind 43

Resources 81

About the Author. 83

Notes 87

Dedication

I would like to dedicate this book to My grandmother Jacqueline Humphrey for igniting the Enduring the Course Model in Me. My mother Yolanda Humphery-Monroe for being my "rider" in every situation. "The People", My husband Brian Hull and my wonderful wonderful friends for putting up with me, believing in me, supporting me, and loving me!

Foreword

It was such a privilege and honor to read the new release, Enduring The Course. This power-packed informational mental health resource is going to be huge for many families and professionals!

The introduction is very strong with two well known stories but from the perspective of mental health.

The author provides valuable information and she keeps the engagement of the reader by using real life examples, transparency and or illustrations.

EBONYJAE, LISW-S

The author created a resource that is simplified, clear, and concise. She avoided using mental health lingo to ensure the reader would be able to understand and make the best decision possible, if applicable.

This book gives you a greater understanding of a therapist, psychiatrist and psychologist.

The author made it easy for me to connect and I personally felt I learned a lot of helpful information as a mother of two strong young children. I personally loved the genuineness of the author and if I needed assistance to this capacity, she would definitely be my first choice.

This book is not long or overwhelming it is perfect for everyone with children!

Kendrea Steward

CEO | STEWARD PUBLISHING, LTD.

www.stewardpublishing.org

Enduring the Course

A guide for parents to increase their understanding, reducing stigma, and expand intervention options when experiencing mental health concerns.

E B O N Y " E B O N Y J A E " H U L L

Therapist/Licensed Clinical Social Worker

Introduction

> "There is more than one way to skin a cat"
>
> —Unknown

This book is designed to aid parents and families in feeling supported and providing tools to help our children to be able to successfully tackle mental health challenges. I want educators and my peers to feel equipped to support the families they are working with. Here I plan to increase understanding, reduce stigma and expand intervention options for people experiencing mental health concerns. By enlightening parents and educators the whole community will be benefited.

> It is easier to build strong children than repair broken Adults
> —Fredrick Douglas

There are only a few things I've realized that you don't have to directly teach children and one of them is to lie. Think about a two-year old you catch writing on the wall, you ask them if they did it and with crayon in hand they say "no". You think and may even say out loud "this two-year old is caught red handed yet he sat here and lied, now where he get that from?" More than likely that two-year old has been popped or told something like "that's a nono", which has taught them about disappointment and maybe fear but at this point no one has actual coached or encourage them to actually lie. Now, don't get me wrong there are parents that teach their children, sometimes lying is ok (most times this does not happen at two). For example, when you get an unwanted phone call and you tell your child to say you are not here. This is different. What I'm talking about, the is the little kid that now understand that actions result in consequence. They have automatically learned that some things I do will get me in trouble, so to avoid trouble I will say "I didn't do that" (equaling a lie).

It is my desire that this book will teach you that negative behaviors and characteristics are learned. I wanted to give you two extreme examples in order to drive this point home. These are real stories that happened in my hometown Cleveland, Ohio not even 10 years ago. The first person I knew personally, for protection I'll just call him MadDogg. I met MadDogg in the summer of 1999. I was 18 and has just started hanging back in my old neighborhood, (shout out to EC, particularly Marlos, Van buren and Roxford) when I met him. Her expressed his interest in me and I began to inquire about him. I learned he had recently been released from jail. No other information was offered. This was "normal" for the hood so I asked no other questions. In other words, going to jail was far from unusual, almost all the boys I knew had been arrested for selling drugs, so I assumed that was his charge also (Hey, the internet wasn't what it is today in 2020 and when you know better you do better!).

MadDogg and I began to hang out for a few weeks. He was nice to the kids in the neighborhood and almost always had a smile on his face. He was pretty quiet but when he talked he liked to make others laugh. He had some questionable ways about him, and I quickly learned he wasn't for me. There was nothing personal or special that happened so moving on was quick and easy. A few years go by and MadDogg and I cross paths again at a few family functions not interacting more than a "what's up" but for some reason that smile looked different.

A few years go by and me a MadDogg cross paths again at a few family functions not interacting more than a "what's up" but for some reason that smile looked different. It felt creepy.

Fast forward, 2013 hits, I'm pregnant with my last daughter. I was in my last semester of undergrad, tired, swallow and hungry. I sit down on the couch and I'm watching the news. This was something I very rarely did but I was so exhausted I didn't even bother to change the TV. As I sit there, mind-drifting to my to do list, a story comes on talking about 3 young women that had been murdered in East Cleveland. That especially caught my attention; since I know people that still live there. I was hoping that none of the young ladies was someone I knew. It wasn't. I felt sad but relieved at the same time. The story continues and they reveal the suspect was MadDogg. The name didn't ring a bell to me which also was a relief. Remember. I told you our encounter was brief and nowhere near personal, so I never even knew his last name.

And then they showed him. He's on trial for murder and he's smiling! That same sinister smile that had creeped me out years earlier and with tears in my eyes and tired, hungry and swallow as I was, I jumped up and got on my knees and thanked God. I felt a sense of sadness for those families but the next thought that came to my mind was: "I could have been one of those girls' years earlier."

As the weeks progressed and the news coverage continued, my social work instincts began to kick it. I remember thinking to myself this is about his mother. Now I never met her (unfortunately, in 2019 she was murdered by MadDogg stepson) but for some reason I started to recall the last time I hung out with MadDogg. He asked me to take him to her house. I take him to this apartment in Shaker and I waited in my car. He comes back out after some time and he started to cry. I was confused and concerned, asking him what was wrong. He told me, "I need a place to stay and she told me I couldn't stay with her because she had a boyfriend." He said something to the effect of her choosing a man over him again. Of course, in the moment I felt bad for him, but I was 18 living with my parents there was nothing I could do for him. We drove across town in silence I dropped him off and that was it for us.

The second person is unfortunately being brought up because of a murder also. He is known as the Cleveland Facebook killer; so again, for privacy that's the name we will use. In 2017, he murdered an elderly gentleman we will call, Mr. G, who was walking home Easter day, on FB live (FB live is where you can record something and it is instantly accessible by others). After he shot Mr. G, he said in the video that he was going to continue to kill people until his mother or until this particular lady called him.

He stated several times in the live that this was happening because of "her". He said that he had tried to talk to others, and they brushed him off. He said that he has been the "butt of others jokes, and now I have snapped."

In this case I don't know either one of these gentlemen, but I do know someone that is very closely related to this story. I met this person in 2019, and Facebook killer came up. This person didn't go into details and neither did I ask. He was relevant to the history the person was talking about, but the incident was not.

Now at this time, I'm a Licensed Independent Social Worker, in other words I sleep, eat and think people. So, I had questions but not what people normally ask, I wanted to know how was the Facebook Murder aside from what we learned about him from this tragedy?

This person detailed their experience of him being, caring and loving but with flaws of course. Nothing that stood out of him being aggressive, crazy, let alone a killer. I remember saying to that person, the sad thing is the world will never know that side of him.

You may be still wondering thinking: this is not what I bought this book for. Or, I don't come here for a Cleveland history of murder. *By the way, isn't that the city who has the not so great football team?* Yeap, but we're also the city that won one of the best most intense basketball championships in 2016. Ok, I digress.

With both stories I want you to think back to what I said in the beginning "It is my desire with this book to teach you that negative behaviors and characteristics are learned. And just like negative behaviors are learned so are positive ones". I will venture to say that neither one of these men were born killers, life happened, they just felt this was the way to respond.

Let's get to what your here for!

A Basis of Understanding

There is no excuse for the actions of Maddogg or Facebook killer! However, it is my belief that just like the two-year old, life experiences dictate our actions. With this in mind, we must consider the current buzz word, mental illness and its effects.

Disclaimer by no means am I saying that having a diagnosis will lead you down the path of your child being a murderer! What I am saying is that mental illness, left untreated will create a dangerous course for the individual and the people connected!

Let's start with Google's definition of mental illness- are health conditions involving changes in emotion, thinking or behavior (or a combination of these). Mental illnesses are associated with distress and/or problems functioning in social, work or family activities.

In layman's terms, Mental illness is behavioral or mental patterns that cause significant distress or impairment of a person's functioning. What does this mean? When your mood, thinking and behavior is affected in a negative way for an extended period.

HOW DO I KNOW THAT MY CHILD'S BEHAVIOR IS A MENTAL ILLNESS NOT THEM JUST BEING BAD?

Your 9-year old doesn't want to go to school. Every day he comes home crying, and every morning he begs to be homeschooled. You see the panic in his eyes. You know it's real. But is he just a kid who doesn't like school, or is it something more? Is this what anxiety looks like?

Almost daily, at least 3 times a week, your kindergarten teacher calls you with reports that your little girl is talking excessively, unable to sit calmly during circle time and is just constantly being in motion. You think she's only 6. What 6-year old can sit still for hours at a time? Then you review your day at home and how she struggles to even sit still at mealtime. If you are like most parents, you next thought is not maybe my child needs therapy. Actually, your first thought is probably that in either situation is my child being picked on or singled out?

A recent study released in JAMA Pediatrics Trusted Source estimated that 7.7 million children — roughly 16.5 percent nationwide — have at least one mental health disorder. Yet, only about 50% of those children are receiving any kind of treatment from a mental health professional.

WHY IS THIS?

The first reason is how could they be treated if parents aren't aware the issue is more than misbehavior? Each child is different, and each generation is even more different than the prior one, so even if you've raised children before you may still find it hard to know the difference. Therefore, this is not one size fits all.

Let me put your mind at ease, we understand these statistics aren't because there isn't help available or because parents don't care. My belief is that, parents just do not know. I have spent years and thousands of dollars in order to inquire this knowledge therefore it is understandable that you wouldn't fully recognize certain behaviors as symptoms of true mental illness, as opposed to just "being sad" or "getting nervous" or "shy".

Before we move on, let us address the elephants in the room. There have been major advancements on how the country views mental health, but make no mistake there is still a long way to go. People are still discouraged and frankly scared to admit that themselves or someone connected to them may have a mental health issue. Pulse. Take a deep breath. You are already one step ahead, by picking up this book. By the end of this book you will have the tools to point you in the right direction as to what you next step should be.

There are three parts to all of us: your thoughts, your feelings, and your behaviors. When one of those are out of sync, the lines get crossed and things go haywire. We are unable to express ourselves correctly. Here you can learn which of your child's wires are crossed and maybe even why.

Realizing there might be something different about your child, will cause you to have many feelings. When you're feeling this way, I want you to take a step back.

Think back for a moment. In most cases, when we are preparing to be first time parents, we read everything we can on parenting. We ask people that are parents already and the doctors a million and one questions. And if your anything like me, you signed up for parenting classes, lamaze and even doulas or midwives. So, I want you to go back to that place of openness. Making sure that what you are seeing is age appropriate behaviors and not mental health issues, has to be established immediately. If you are unsure a good starting point is your child pediatricians.

You probably picked up this book because you feel that "normal" discipline or consequences are not working? What you deem as age appropriate punishment is no longer effective? Here could be some of these behaviors that may be present (Note- This is not an all-inclusive list):

- Persistent sadness — two or more weeks

- Withdrawing from or avoiding social interactions

- Hurting oneself or talking about hurting oneself

- Talking about death or suicide

- Outbursts or extreme irritability

- Out-of-control behavior that can be harmful

- Drastic changes in mood, behavior or personality

- Changes in eating habits

- Loss of weight

- Difficulty sleeping

- Frequent headaches or stomachaches

- Difficulty concentrating

- Changes in academic performance

- Avoiding or missing school

- Trouble following multi step directions

You take your child for their check up and find out for once, you are right. The doctor confirms these behaviors are not on track with normal development for your child's age. They then refer you to a mental health specialist and you begin to panic.

Mental health and the Church

In my practice, I pride myself on assisting clients through a Holistic approach. What this means, not only do we address your mental health needs, we look at the whole person.

The support you get from me will also consider your physical, emotional, social and spiritual well-being. Therefore, I would remiss by not addressing mental issues and the church. Let me first reference this, by saying I identify as a Christian and believe in the doctrine that goes with it. Secondly, by no means is this book being written to place blame or tear down anyone especially not the Church! With being said, that doesn't mean I agree with everything the church does.

If you have been to church or know someone in the church, you have probably heard something like "all you have to do is pray and God will make away." While this is true, one of my favorite scriptures is James 2:18, NASB: "But someone may well say, "You have faith and I have works; show me your faith without the works, and I will show you my faith by my works." I have heard this preached many ways, but for the purpose of staying on topic, we're going to go with my interpretation. The way I would like to apply this scripture is this: we believe (faith) that God is a Way Maker, and we know that in order to get results action (works) have to be taken. Prayer by definition "is a solemn request for help or expression of thanks addressed to God." God has entrusted people, wait not just people, but other believers like myself, who have credentials to provide you with support. So, we can "get you together" through scripture and theory. I absolutely believe in the power of prayer, but I have petitioned God and in His answer, it was something I had to do also.

Think about it like this, have you thought to yourself, "'I need a job" and your phone rang and on the other end there was a job offer? If so, then you can skip this chapter. I personally have never gotten a job without one of these things, communicating (action) that I was looking for a job, filling out an application (works), or having an interview (deeds) along with my prayer (which normally goes something like this: God if it is your will then please open this door...). My prayers include Him guiding me and/or sending me people to guide me in the direction I should go. In other words, I like to see it as God and I partnering to get things done. I don't just do what I want to do. It is my belief that prayer is the first part and the second part is hearing how God tells you to move.

The stigma attached to mental health is very prevalent even in the church. I know a person that went up for prayer at church one Sunday morning for healing and was told something like, healing was not taking place because they did not have enough faith. Again, this is false. Lets go back to what I said above, there is levels to this: PRAYER, FAITH, and then ACTION. Now let me be clear there are times where the action God tells you to take is to "be still" but the fact is you are still doing something.

HOW DOES THIS CONNECT WITH MENTAL HEALTH?

You might be thinking EbonyJae and her rabbit trials, (now y'all know how church people are, lol), but stay with me.

In my experience we sometimes get caught in the myth that once you become "saved" you're not affected by the things of the world. FALSE. What most will tell you is once they have confessed and committed to being intentional about doing things God's way is when it seems "all hell begins to break loose." As Christians we are not immune to anything including mental health. Mental health hit each and every person that lives in some shape or form.

Because of that myth in past times this has allowed us as the church to not fully (if at all address this.) Even though we know that not addressing something does not make it go away.

BUT THERE IS GOOD NEWS.

My actual favorite scripture is Jeremiah 29:11, NIV (For I know the plans I have for you," declares the LORD, "plans to prosper you and not to harm you, plans to give you hope and a future.) A definition of the word plan is: a detailed proposal for doing or achieving something. What this scripture says to me is that because of God's plan for my life and yours that even when we are struggling we can find hope in things can get better.

I remember when I got the call that my pops was unresponsive and we needed to get to the hospital. When we got there my mom was distraught because he was in a medically induced comma, but I wasn't. Not even a year earlier I walked into a hospital room where my mom was unresponsive and ended up in a medically induced comma for five weeks. So I had seen the power of prayer and it was my belief that God could heal him. Well that didn't happen, he passed less than a week later. God could have absolutely allowed him to stay alive but what kinda of life would that left him? My realization was even though I wanted him here with me, what better place than to be with God, Remember?

This just reminds me personally of how much love God has for us that in our worst time He still has the best for us.

I added this part of the book to hopefully connect how mental health affects us all. Remember, the title of this book is Enduring the Course, and with that in mind there will be times the road is bumpy and as Christian we are called to seek out Christ which includes the church.

But even in hope there is still some issue.

The Bible tells us to seek wise counsel, so we then run to the church. The problem is in most cases the church is not fully equipped to assist with mental health. Too often when mental health issues come up or are spoken about in the church it is connected with a demon attached. Who want to admit or believe that they have a demon in them? I sure don't. Therefore even in the 21st century many are afraid to speak about what is bothering them mentally. How is it the place we go to for hope is often the place we find the most hurt? Churches have allowed mental health to be taboo for far too long. I honestly do not believe that it was intentional but that does negate the facts.

I know that this guide is to help you navigate your child through the process but if you are a believer there is no way to do this with out your spiritual parts being in tactics also. There are going to be times that the only thing that saves you or your child is something supernatural, but you will not lean on the church, if you don't feel it is ok. Let's not forget that hopefully one day your child will grow up and as the parents the better we are the better off they can be.

Just like any other situation your child's issues will feel unbearable at times and you will need a place to softly land. It is my desire that this book is a start for the entire Body of Christ to recognize that we have played a part in allowing our people to suffer in silence and that is not what God has intended for us. It is my personal opinion that this is how the enemy has been allowed to cause havoc. We have been led to believe that prayer is enough and we when do not see change we believe this how it was meant to be. That is simply not true.

WHAT CAN WE DO AS A CHURCH?

First, we have to admit that mental health issues are real. I hear often, "Where was all these diagnosis years ago?" My is answer is, they have been here all along, we just have a better understanding. Sometimes people will continue to disagree. Then, I break down the diagnosis really is saying and that is simple, in which the person is emotionally or psychologically distressed for whatever reason. That usually stops the disagreement.

Secondly, if you are in leadership in the church and someone comes to you struggling with mental health issues offer prayer and your wisdom but recognize that if you are not clinically trained you can unintentionally make things worse. While we know the Bible say "spare the rod spoil the child" somethings will not be corrected with physical discipline. Don't disregard them or just leave it there. Offer scriptures they can read but also normalize seeking professional help.

Lastly, just like you have life groups or even AA/NA meetings team up with a Mental Health expert and offer services to your congregation. *Shameless plug alert* (Enduring the Course is not just a book we are a nonprofit organization that would love to see if we could support your church, our contact information is in the back of the book). I was taught that churches are the equivalent to a hospital but for the soul. Churches are often the place where people go to when they have tried everything else. Let's allow church to be a one stop shop.

Managing the Mind

While efforts are being made to normalize mental health treatment, there is still a huge stigma attached to seeking mental health treatment. You may begin to feel like somehow this is your fault. Maybe you feel you have failed as a parent or you may fear what others will say or think. Let me reassure you, according to CDC.gov "Mental health disorders are the most common diseases of childhood. Of the 74.5 million children in the United States, an estimated 17.1 million have or have had a psychiatric disorder — more than the number of children with cancer, diabetes, and AIDS combined." Now that you know you are not alone let's move on.

LEARNING THE DIFFERENCE

The best thing you can do at this point is to follow the doctor's order and reach out to a mental health professional. There are many resources available to support you and your child through this and I will break some of them down for you in this book for better understanding. It is important for you to realize the earlier your child diagnosis and appropriately treated the better.

WE ARE READY FOR TREATMENT, BUT DO WE GO TO A PSYCHIATRIST, PSYCHOLOGIST OR A THERAPIST?

Unknown to most there are differences between psychiatrist and psychologist and a therapist. To make matters even more confusing, these aren't the only mental health professionals you can choose from. There are mental health counselors, social workers, nurses and nurse practitioners, and others who deal with issues of mental health. Here we will stick to explaining these 3, psychiatrist, psychologist or a therapist.

PSYCHIATRISTS are licensed medical physicians, they can prescribe medications, and often spend much of their time involved with patients discussing mediation management and treatment course planning.

PSYCHOLOGISTS focus substantially on psychotherapy and treating emotional regulation and mental health symptoms by utilizing behavioral modification techniques. Psychologists are also qualified to conduct psychological testing, which is essential in evaluating an individual's mental health state and determining the most effective treatment course.

THERAPIST (also interchangeably with the terms counseling) narrows in on specific issues and is designed to help address an individual's problem, such as anxiety or attention issues. The focus may include problem solving or be on learning specific coping techniques to avoid problem areas. Additional services provided by clinician include psychotherapy, emotional regulation, as well as behavioral modification techniques.

I have an appointment what can I expect?

The first step will be to complete an assessment (when meeting with a psychiatrist this may include medical exam). The assessment maybe done with the person you will be working with or it may be done by someone else and then the info will be passed on to the person your family will be treat by. This is typically the longest (and what some say is the most annoying) meeting you will have. It can be done in one session but in most cases will happen over multiple sessions. During this process, you and your child will be asked a lot of questions. They will probably separate you two at points in order to get information that maybe uncomfortable to discuss in front of each other.

From this point on I will discuss from a therapist (therapist and counselor may be used interchangeably) point of view since this is the area, I am credential in. Each therapist may conduct the appointment differently but there are a few standard things that will be discussed.

- History of physical or emotional trauma your child has experienced

- Family history of physical and mental health

- Review of symptoms and general concerns with parents

- Timeline of child's developmental progress

- Academic history

- Insurance requirements

- HIPPA compliance and safety

- Treatment plan

Gathering this information is how things are ruled out in order for your child to find a proper diagnosis. Diagnosing mental illness in children can take time because young children may have trouble understanding or expressing their feelings, and normal development varies. Your child's diagnosis may change or be refined over time.

WHY IS SO MUCH HISTORY NECESSARY? THAT'S THE PAST.

Remember earlier I mentioned the three parts of a person? Your thoughts, feelings and your behaviors. The therapeutic process encompasses working on every part of the person in treatment. Our history absolutely dictates our future. We do thing the way we do them because of things we have experience. This may not even be things we've experienced firsthand.

Have you ever done something just because that's how your mother or even your grandmother did it? There have been several times when someone has asked me "why did you do it like that?", and several times the answer has simply been because "I don't know, that's how my mother did it." Other times we don't do things because people close to us have been negativity effected by them. We then are afraid the same or even worse will happen to you.

Our history can provide us with insight into the origin, thereby increasing awareness and understanding. By revealing things from your past, it can disclose the whys to the person's thoughts feelings and behaviors.

PAPERWORK IS DONE, WHAT WILL A SESSION LOOK LIKE?

After getting passed the stigma of treatment, parents next concern is what will be required of both then and their child. A common question is, "will I have to put my child on medication?" Medication is not for everyone. Medication should always be viewed as an option if suggested. Medication is to aid in stabilizing your child. Side note: Therapist do not prescribe medication, and Psychologist can only prescribe certain medications. Therefore, most often if you are working with either of the two mentioned above and your child needs medicine, they may be referred to a Psychiatrist. Even then there are still other options your child can benefit from and that is where Psychologists and Therapists come in. Therapists most often uses a method called Psychotherapy or talk therapy, to address your child's symptoms.

Psychotherapy focuses on a broad range of issues such as a child's patterns of thinking and behavior that affect the way that person interacts with the world. Depending on the specific type of psychotherapy that is being used, the goal is to help people feel better equipped to manage stresses, understand patterns in their behavior that may interfere with reaching personal goals, have more satisfying relationships, and better regulate their thinking and emotional responses to stressful situations.

Ultimately, the purpose of therapy will help you cope, manage, and move through situations that cause them anger, grief, depression, and other emotional burdens. During Psychotherapy your child will learn ways to improve their communication and listening skills at every level and in any area of life.

In the session, the Therapist may play games with your child. As a parent you may see them for example, playing CandyLand and wonder how this is beneficial. In reality, your child could be learning skills like waiting their turn, being a team play or even focusing. There are countless of activities and techniques that can be used in order to address your child's symptoms. You may also be required to participate in session also.

All types of therapeutic pay may be a part of the session. As a parent you may see this and wonder how this is beneficial. In reality your child could be learning skills like waiting their turn, being a team play or even focusing. There are countless of activities and techniques that can be used in order to address your child's symptoms. You may also be required to participate in session also. When I am developing a treatment plan with the family, I included at least one goal the child wants to work on, one goal the parent wants to work on, and one goal I feel is necessary for progress of every child.

Parents committing to participate is crucial. This could be done as a check in before and after the session with the client, a phone call, a session where the child is present or a session where the child is not present. This is an important part of your child's process. In order for you to support your child you need to know what is being worked on and sometimes you need to be taught skills to reinforce things your child is learn in therapy.

WHAT EXPECTATIONS WILL I NEED TO MEET AS A PARENT AND WHAT WILL NOT HAPPEN IN THERAPY?

This maybe the hardest chapter to read but I believe it will be the most helpful. I will intentionally be direct in this chapter, because I believe that this is the most important part of the book. It may cause you to feel uncomfortable and maybe even challenged. This section may cause you to be ready to close the book at this point and that's okay, but I am strongly encouraging you not to. I give this same information to parents face to face on a regular basis and not once have I had a parent discontinue services with me after these types of conversations.

Therapy can be long term or short term depending on the diagnosis. I personally am a result driven person, so I prefer short term therapy. What this means is that I like it best when I can measure my clients progress and I am able to track this as goals complete through their treatment plan. This will vary from client to client, but one of the common tasks is measured by something established by me and the parent and typically the child is rewarded with something. In other words, the parent (or guardian) has to be present and has to participate.

WHAT THERAPY IS NOT?

THERAPY NOR MEDICATION WILL NOT FIX YOUR CHILD! Let me say that again. THERAPY NOR MEDICATION WILL NOT FIX YOUR CHILD! Medication and therapy are tools to aid a person in being the healthiest version of themselves and living the best life possible. Too often parents will say that "therapy did not work" or " all they did was talked and played". The reality is that talking and playing allows the therapist to teach the child a beneficial skill on their level.

For example, with my teens we play card games a lot such as Uno. Uno? How is that therapeutic or teaching a skill. I'm glad you asked. Let's say my client has been diagnosed with ADHD for example, playing a card game will require them to focus, they will have to stop and think before they react which works on impulsivity. Now, let's use that same game for a younger child who is struggling with following directions or speaking without raising their hand. By playing this type of game they learn that they have to wait their turn and they are required to go by the rules in order to continue the game. Along with this we will have a discussion to tie into how they can transfer these skills into everyday life.

Now to the point of "all they did was talk". I want you to think about your best friend. What are some qualities that make them your best friend? Do you say things like they are a good listener, or you can trust them with your secrets? I hope so. While the Therapist will not be your child's best friend, they will need to have some of the same qualities.

I don't know if parents, expect the conversations to be a certain way or not but I am here to tell you, if we did it the way you do it then we would get nowhere.

Depending on where we are in the process and what your child is experiencing, we may spend some of our session talking about Drake's latest song, or which couple we think will stay together on 90-day fiancé. You may be thinking "you mean to tell me this is therapeutic?" Yes! It absolutely is. This can be part of our rapport build process. Just like your best friend, we have to learn about your child's interest in order to relate to them. Another reason why this maybe happening is because we may have just discussed something really heavy, so this conversation can server a means to lighten the activity we just completed. I never leave a client in a heavy place, if I can help it.

I want you to think again to Maddogg and the facebook killer, in both cases they acted alone, yet I can guarantee that giving the opportunity they will blame their actions as a result of something that was done to them. Under the right circumstance what you would learn is there is some truth to this. Their actions were a result of them never being properly treated. When things go wrong, we often like to blame someone or something else. Again, there is some truth to this. We are products of our environment, it up to us as parent or adults to make the necessary changes.

Here is where it might get tough. The first thing I want you to think about is have you contribute to your child's symptoms? I will venture to say that your answer should be Yes. But, "aren't some diagnosis due to genetics?", you might be thinking. If so, "how could that be my fault?". Yes. Some diagnosis are due to genetics, but there are contributing factors that can increase symptoms. The reason we are starting with YOU, is if you did not know the issue, how could you provide a solution? You can't.

Has your child ever shared a school problem with you? Your first instinct was to go to the school or reach out to the teacher to try and resolve it? Sure, you have, and what is wrong with this? Nothing, if done properly. I cannot tell you how many clients I have tell me about a situation that they never tell their parents and when I ask why. The universal answer is, "I know how my parent is and I do not want to see them get in trouble."

We are supposed to protect and advocate for our children but if done incorrectly, the wrong message can be sent. We say things like "if someone hurts you, you tell me, and I will hurt them." In the same breath, we teach our kids there is consequences for hurting others. Therefore, your child may equate that to meaning if I tell my parent that someone hurt me, my parent is going to hurt them and go to jail and I will be taken away. You may see this as farfetched, but I am telling you, I have been told this by several clients.

Another way you may have contributed to you child symptoms is by the bad habits you have learned. My family has this running joke about how at one point we had dinner for every occasion. We joke, if you lost a pound, we're having dinner; if you gained a pound, we're having dinner. Because of this dynamic, I have now learned that I am an emotional eater and my mood dictates my food choices often. When I'm happy I can make better food choices. When I have a negative feeling, let's say sadness, I usually choose something that fattening or high in sugar or what most call it is "comfort foods". When we think about this example, the intention of us getting together was not to eat but to be supportive to each other's life changes good or bad. Yet, I've subconsciously I sometimes have a unhealthy relationship with food.

The good thing is since am aware of this, I have been able to put things in place so that when I began to crave foods that are unhealthy, I look at "Why" first. Where am I emotionally? Or do I just want ice cream today because it's hot and a summer day? Then I go from there. If I realize that this craving is the result of a negative emotion, then I try to do something else that makes me feel better, like calling a friend or watch a tv show I like instead of allowing the food item to make me feel better. Without having things in place, I could have become overweight and/or have other health issues. Not to mention, passing these unhealthy ways and down to my children.

The last way you may contribute to your child's symptoms, is by you being the problem. Yes, your child's symptoms maybe because of YOU! As a therapist, I have never said this directly to a parent, but I have thought it. The truth of the matter is parents sometimes YOU are the problem. Let me be honest, I probably didn't have to state the YOU as the parent might be the PROBLEM so many times here, but it feels so good to say! This is not to discredit you as a parent, I can say this in confidence because I too have been the problem.

As parents we may believe that since we are doing the best we can or as I stated earlier this how the previous generation did and "we turned out alright" (or did we?, we'll save that answer for the next book lol). Even in our best efforts our children are affected by the environments we put them in. Environment can include inside the home, outside the home, family members, family dynamics, church, schools, or neighborhoods. In other word, without the right tools our kids can ultimately struggle more than they have too. Unfortunately, the finger can still be pointed back at us, since very rarely does the child have a choice in the matter.

The next way the parent can be the problem when we become overwhelmed and can't think straight, we unintentionally create unrealistic expectations. We may begin to feel that the child should just complete chores and do all their schoolwork on time and become more frustrated when they don't. Other times we have not dealt with our own issues that then interfere with our parenting and responding to children in a positive way. This may look like yelling when we should/could address the matter in a calmer fashion. Then there are the times or parents who simply where never taught how to be a parent and when adding mental illness (yours or your child's) on top of that can cause a world of challenges.

I told you this would be the hardest chapter, especially if you see yourself in one or more of the examples listed above. Maybe you're thinking, it wasn't that bad especially since I don't do any of those things. Well parents the book could only be but so long, with more example I'm sure you would have found yourself in there somewhere. But the purposes of the chapter was not to condemn but to bring awareness, understanding and ways to make corrections (interventions). It is my hope that is what you got from this chapter.

LET'S REVIEW WHAT COULD BE EXPECTED FROM YOU AS THE PARENT:

- Once working with the therapist, keep all appointments when possible even if "nothing is going on". Things can change in a moment, but if you feel like your child has made major improvements, have a conversation with your counselor and work together to make adjustments. Stopping prematurely can be damaging to the progress that has been made.

- Be positive and supportive. If you are negative about therapy, it may interfere with your child's perception and therefore it won't work.

- Communicate with the therapist on what you feel is working and not working. Voice your concerns but be open to trust and try things that are out of your comfort zone. Don't be afraid to change therapist if nothing is working or you feel this person is not a good fit, but do not give up on counseling all together.

- Understand that it is not the counselor's job to discipline your child it is your job. If you need help, then let the counselor know that way they can offer things you can do to get the results you want.

- Don't expect the therapist or your child to give you complete details of every session. While you will be privy to most information, your child needs to feel safe to express themselves without feeling like they will be in trouble.

- Know that you will be required to makes some changes in order to help with the process. If your child's Therapist is unable to incorporate designated times to address your concerns of your child's symptoms, consider family counseling to deal with uneasiness. Don't be afraid to ask your child's mental health professional for advice on how to respond to your child and handle difficult behavior.

- You are not always right, and the counselor will not always agree with you. If you had all the answers you would be here. It sounds harsh, but it is true. You may be a good parent, but you may need to do thing differently in order to decrease your child's symptoms.

- Be open to participating in session when requested, it maybe the breakthrough your child needs. Be honest. You don't have to worry about being judged.

- Don't stop treatment permanently. If you find that treatment (weather its medication, talk therapy or any other treatment) is not working be sure to express this. You may have inside information that will assist with figuring out what adjustments need to be made.

- Enroll in parent training programs, or even online groups particularly designed for parents of children with a mental illness. Explore stress management techniques to help you respond calmly.

- Seek ways to relax and have fun with your child. Praise your child's strengths and abilities.

- Work with your child's school to secure necessary support. And make sure to take time for yourself!

Just because you think your child need therapy does not mean this is the case. Your child may be struggling but does not meet the diagnostic criteria for therapy. Or if you have a teenage who does not want to go to therapy, forcing them will not be productive. You may have to reason with them to give it a try or you may need to find a therapist or some other support that can provide you with the tools to help your child.

Consider going to therapy for you, some therapist may require as part of the child's treatment plan every so often the parents come alone and learn techniques to be able to positively contribute to the process which may include making sure you as the parent is practicing good self-care.

Last but not least. In fact it is one of the most important factors in this book. AS A PARENT YOU MUST PRACTICE SELF-CARE. (OK, I'm done yelling at you.) I know this is easier said than done but it is a must! You might be thinking "what is self-care" or "I don't have time for self-care." Self-care will look different for everyone but it's necessary. How I define self-care is internally doing something for YOURSELF! Here are a few things you can get started with:

- Finding a hobby (this could include reading books, listening to a podcast, going to Youtube University)

- Scheduling time with friend(s) without kids

- Making time to date your partner and/or yourself

- Taking an uninterrupted bath

- Getting a makeover

- Take a vacation

- Taking a day off work without telling anyone and just sleep or binge watch something

- Take a class

- Join a Zoom and learn something new (We're in a Global Pandemic) There is a Zoom for practically everything and a lot of things are free or discounted

- Start a workout regimen

- See a Therapist or other Mental Health Provider specifically for yourself (I hope you didn't think you would be off the hook lol)

This is a very small list but it is major. You have to make time for you or you will do more harm than good. With stress comes poor decision making. We become impulsive, snippy, angry, and just off our game. This is how a start or increase to addiction happens. Things like substance abuse and overeating are birthed from not using proper coping skills when we become overwhelmed (this includes smoking weed to calm your nerves, having a few glasses of wine to help you sleep, or eating several snacks because you are sad.) I recognize that life is busy but self-care needs to be non-negotiable, it has to be prioritized right with eating, pooping and sleeping. One example I use with clients all the time is what happens if a person is unable to use the bathroom for an extended period of time. Do you know? It can start coming out of your mouth. Disgusting right? Of course but true. Stress is the same way. Suppressing or not addressing your stress in a healthy way will force them to come out in a negative way that will impact you and the child.. * This book may appear to be mainly speaking to Parents but actually it and should and could be applied to and by everyone. Think about this, if you have ever been on an airplane or even may have even seen it in a movie before taking flight there are some instructions given. One is, (paraphrased) "In an event of an emergency and oxygen masks are needed, put your mask on first before helping someone else, this includes children." Why would you not put your child's mask on first? I'd rather they live. If everyone on the plane thought like that, then it is a possibility that the only survivors would be children. In most cases this would not turn out well because children or (your passed out husband) would not likely make a good survival experience. On the other hand, if you, the adult with life experience, and are conscious, there might be a better chance.

Continue to learn as much about the mental illness as you can. Your mental health professional (MHP) can provide you with education written or verbally. Of course, you can find information on you own as well. Note: that in order to be able to advocate, you should be knowledgeable about your child's mental health struggles.

Time to start you journey of Enduring the Course!

You child may go through several agencies, or private practices until you have determined it is a good fit. This is perfectly okay! Enduring means to continue or long lasting. Treating mental health will be a journey (a course, if you will). In other words, it will take some time in order to get your child to a stable place if diagnosed. If prescribed medication, it may take a few changes to the dosage before you see improvements. I want to reassure you this is normal and part of the process. Think of it like this, when you go to a car lot, would you just see a car, walk in pay for it and leave? No! You are going to look around, test drive it, maybe even spend some time negotiating the price. There is no exact way or timeframe because everyone is different. It may take you a while to accept that your child has a mental illness that may be a part of them for the rest of their life.

You may see your child make major progress and then one day, Boom! There is a setback. I want you to know just like with any other medical condition, some diagnosis will change quick and other will not. The best thing you can do is do what you have done by reading this book, continue to take steps that add to positively improving your child's symptoms.

I READ THIS BOOK AND I STILL DO NOT KNOW IF WE SHOULD SEEK PROFESSIONAL HELP OR NOT?

Review the symptoms listed below, if your child is experiencing one or more symptoms this is a good indicator that seeking more information would be suggested. Therapy is not end all be all, but it has been proven for over 50 years as a means to providing support, encouragement and assisting with helping people to be their best selves.

- Depression

- Excessive use of drugs/Alcohol

- Low energy

- Excessive use of prescriptions

- Low self-esteem

- Blackouts

- Poor concentration

- Physical/ Sexual/Verbal abuse

- Hopelessness

- Spousal abuse issues

- Worthlessness

- Anger/Frustration
- Guilt
- Easily agitated/Annoyed
- Sleep disturbance
- Defies rules
- Thoughts of hurting self
- Blames others
- Thoughts of hurting others
- Cannot hold onto an idea
- Cutting/Self-injurious behaviors
- Divorce/Separation
- Sadness/Loss
- Excessive behaviors

- Grief/Mourning
- Delusions/Hallucinations
- Stress
- Not thinking clearly/Confusion
- Anxiety/Panic
- Isolation/Social withdrawal
- Heart pounding/racing
- Appetite changes (more/less)
- Chest pain
- Restlessness/Difficulty sitting still
- Sweating
- Feeling that you are not real
- Fear of dying

- Lose track of time

- Fear of going crazy

- Unpleasant thoughts that won't go away

- Gambling/Spending

- Health issues

- Relationship issues

- Work stress/issues

- Childhood memories

- School/Academic problems

- Phobias

- Racing thoughts

- Easily distracted

- Legal problems

- Excessive energy

- Difficultly following directions/Staying on task

- Bullies others

- Disrespectful to authority

- Fire-setting behaviors

- Cruelty to animals

Resources

 https://screening.mhanational.org/content/how-common- mental-illness - How common is mental illness?

JAMA Pediatrics – The Science of Child and Adolescent Health. (2014). JAMA Pediatrics, 168(7), 594. doi:10.1001/jamapediatrics.2013.3352

About the Author

Ebony "EbonyJae" Hull, Licensed Independent Social Worker (LISW-S), bringing over ten years of social service experience to uniquely care for people. EbonyJae is the Managing Director of the Nonprofit- Enduring the Course INC., She is highly effective in her clinical work by addressing the emotional, mental, physical, social and spiritual needs of her clients.

EbonyJae, LISW-S

EbonyJae served in the United States Navy for 8 year traveling as far as Kuwait. During this time, her love for people increased due to experience so many people in so many different ways. EbonyJae received both her Bachelor of Social Work and Master of Social Work from the University of Akron. Her professional experience includes working with children, adolescents, adults, and Veterans in a variety of settings such as the home, school and community. Ebony has assisted individuals to become more financially stable, manage mental health, develop healthy relationships, communicate effectively and supported a myriad of family-related issues.

EbonyJae began Enduring the Course Inc., in 2019 to increase understanding, reduce stigma and expand intervention options for people experiencing mental health concerns. Her Positive Parenting and Practitioner Principles were developed to support families, school officials, and other clinicians to positively manage mental health struggles.

Together with Enduring the Course Inc., EbonyJae's areas of expertise includes:

- Education Intervention Diagnosis and Planning

- Adult, Youth and Family Therapy

- Community Engagement

- Healthy Relationships

- Communication Skills

CONNECT WITH EBONYJAE ONLINE:

 online: www.enduringthecourseinc.org

Podcast: Enduring the Course w/EbonyJae

EBONYJAE, LISW-S

🌐 https://anchor.fm/ebonyjae-lisw

ⓕ www.facebook.com/ebonyjaeinfo/

in Enduring the Course https://www.linkedin.com/in/enduring-the-course-inc-07a102ba

✉ mailto:Admin@enduringthecourseinc.org

NOTES

Ebonyjae, LISW-S

Enduring the Course

EBONYJAE, LISW-S

Enduring the Course

EBONYJAE, LISW-S

Enduring the Course

Ebonyjae, LISW-S

Enduring the Course

Ebonyjae, LISW-S

Enduring the Course

Ebonyjae, LISW-S

Made in the USA
Monee, IL
26 October 2020